DO NOT GO GENTLE

POETRY AND PROSE
FROM BEHIND THE WALLS

Edited by
Michael Hogan

Blue Moon Press Inc.
c/o Department of English
University of Arizona
Tucson, Arizona   85721

1977

ACKNOWLEDGMENTS

ROMAN ADRIAN

"Bel Woman" first appeared in *Sun Tracks*, Fall 1976.

PAUL DAVID ASHLEY (1942 – 1975)
    "Prison" first appeared in *Snakeroots*, Fall 1975 under the title of "The Prison."
That poem and all the other Ashley poems included in this anthology have since appeared in a collection of Ashley's work entitled *The Unfinished Man*, copyright 1976 by Baleen Press. Permission to reprint from Ramona Weeks is gratefully acknowledged.

JIM FERRAR
    "Hokusai" and "Two Alternatives To A Moment's Experience" first appeared in *The Greenfield Review*, Summer 1975.

J. CHARLES GREEN (1947 – 1974)
    "Waking Up," "Parole Denial," "Isolation Cell Poem," "Freedom" and "A Day of Notes" all appeared in a collection of Green's work entitled *First Words*, copyright 1975 by The Greenfield Review Press. Permission to reprint from Joseph Bruchac is gratefully acknowledged.

MICHAEL HOGAN
    "One Summer In Charleston" and "Groundhog Day" first appeared in a chapbook entitled *If You Ever Get There, Think Of Me*, copyright 1975 by Michael Hogan. Permission to reprint from Rob Matte of Emerald City Press is gratefully acknowledged.
    "Fish" and "A Quiet Orderly Life" first appeared in *Letters For My Son*, copyright 1975 by Michael Hogan. Permission to reprint from Teo Savory of Unicorn Press is gratefully acknowledged.
    "Rust" first appeared in *The Greenfield Review*, Winter 1976.
    "Poem For My Eighth Year in Prison" first appeared in *The Agni Review*, Winter 1976.

LONNIE L. LANDRUM
    "And Now Out Of Sight" first appeared in *The Youth United Newspaper*, Vol. 6, No. 2.

MICHAEL SMALL
    "A Dream" first appeared in *Fireweed*, Fall 1975. Permission to reprint from Galen Green is gratefully acknowledged.

Cover photo courtesy of Dr. James R. Hastings
Inst. of Atmospheric Physics, University of Arizona

This project is jointly supported by a grant from the Arizona Commission on the Arts and Humanities, a State agency, and the National Endowment for the Arts in Washington, D.C., a Federal agency.

PREFACE

The poems and prose pieces in this anthology were written by members of the Writer's Workshop at the Arizona State Prison between June, 1973, and December, 1975. They are presented in this format because of their literary merit. But behind this presentation is the Writer's Workshop at the Arizona State Prison which goes back more than three years and involves the efforts of many: the farsighted and progressive leadership of the Arizona State Department of Corrections, the continued and enthusiastic support of the Arizona Commission on the Arts and Humanities, the encouragement of the National Endowment for the Arts, and the volunteer services of many writers, teachers, editors, and friends in Arizona and elsewhere.

Without such a degree of cooperation neither this volume nor several others could have existed, nor indeed the Workshop from which they have grown. In Arizona such widespread and sustained cooperation between state institutions and individuals is possible, even in an area as socially and politically sensitive as penology. This volume is one tangible indication of a program which has received a great deal of attention and praise for its ability to provide, within a state prison and at a minimum of public expense, some degree of rehabilitation through the arts. Other indications of this program are the lives of the men who have been or are members of the Writer's Workshop, both those who now live as productive and artistic citizens in the free world, and those who are awaiting the opportunity to do so.

Nearly everyone talks about our contemporary penal system. It is an enormously complex system, but it is often discussed, even in print, in the most simplistic terms. One of the largest problems in connection with that system is recidivism, with its ugly statistics. We call recidivism by various names: some call it part of "psychic death," some call it "chronic criminality," and I call it "the revolving door." But we all know, if we have had any experience with it, that it walks our streets and haunts us, either as our private failure to deal with our own lives, or as our public failure to deal with the lives of those whose future actions will directly affect us.

And so I think I should take this opportunity to congratulate those people who are not merely talking about the problem of recidivism, but attempting to do something about it. Such people are rare.

— I want to congratulate those men who are living in the free world but whose work is represented in this volume, those men who are determined never to return to the Arizona State Prison or any other prison. Certainly they are doing something about the problem of recidivism.

— I want to congratulate the Arizona Department of Corrections and the administration and staff of the Arizona State Prison. Their cheerful cooperation, even in the face of added work and inconvenience, has helped to make the Writer's Workshop possible. As their guest one day each week for more than three years, I rate their hospitality "excellent."

— I want to congratulate the individual members of the Arizona Commission on the Arts and Humanities for their courage, a quality so rare in public life, and for their continuing moral and financial support of the Writer's Workshop.

— I want to congratulate those writers, teachers, students, editors, and friends in Arizona and throughout the country who have given their time, efforts, books, and money to further the long-range program of the Writer's Workshop. Besides those who are mentioned by name in Michael Hogan's "Introduction" to this volume, I want to congratulate and acknowledge the efforts of John Moran, Harold Cardwell, John Wright, Tom Cobb, Joe Karol, Vincent Wehrman, Shelley Cohn, Jerry Yoshitomi, John Levy, Rex Veeder, and James Livingston.

I can congratulate each of you, but I have no right to thank you. Those who have the right to thank you will do so and are doing so in terms of the lives they lead. But I join you in saying we have done what we could in spite of difficulties, both public and private. We have attempted to grapple, in the small way which is available to us, with the problem of recidivism; and we have dealt directly with those people most involved. We have not waited for some promised Utopia nor wasted our time complaining about public apathy. We have attempted to work within the framework of the present system to improve the quality of life which is possible for us and for others. And we will continue to do so.

To those who have nothing but criticism for our often imperfect efforts, we can suggest that it is easier to curse the darkness than to light the small candle which might be found in one's own pocket. And each of us can offer this quotation: "Show me your faith without your works, and I will show you my faith by my works." No one can say more.

Richard Shelton
Director
Writer's Workshop

INTRODUCTION

Whenever someone tells me he is serving "easy time" in a maximum security prison, I feel a little sorry for him. "Easy time" means simply that one has cut himself off from the world. He has accepted the prison walls as the boundaries of his universe and substituted the gray life of non-feeling for the bright and colorful existence of being an open and sensitive human being alive on this earth. I can understand why he has done that.

When he first came to prison there was a shock. He had lost his job, his position in the community, the respect of his friends and the support of his relatives. His horizons, once as limitless as any young man's, suddenly shrank to the confines of the prison compound. The small freedoms he once took for granted were lost, many irrevocably.

If he was young when he entered the prison, he was probably intimidated by older, stronger cons. Possibly, he was assaulted or sexually abused, or equally likely, he seriously injured someone himself to avoid being brutalized. Within a year or two his wife left him or his girl stopped writing. Despair, remorse, self-pity, disgust, the interminable boredom and daily anxiety of cellblock life began taking its toll. He doubted that he could keep his faculties intact if he didn't find a way to stop thinking about it all, stop feeling the things he was feeling.

So he turned to drugs and floated around in a gray haze in which one day was much like any other. He manipulated, dealt, and in his turn abused other young cons. He cut all ties between himself and his family. He gave up on life outside.

Gradually, he no longer felt remorse. Self-pity, disgust, and even rage evaporated in the static world of cellblock life. He settled back and did his time. The days passed quickly and serving time became "easy."

The fact that he seldom laughed any more did not bother him. Or, the fact that he felt incapable of true affection, unmoved by tears, blind to the rising of the sun or to the sparrow perched outside the cellblock window. He had surrendered these things for the psychic death of non-feeling. The pain, the terrible remorse and anxiety and self-disgust were gone. The fact that so much else passed as well was not even noticed as the years went by.

The writings collected in this book are by men who fought against this psychic death, who raged "against the dying of the light." Each one did it in his own unique way and so the poems are not set out in sections, but merely arranged by author. Each group of poems describes a way of seeing, a way of feeling, and a way of being that is unique to each poet.

Many of these strong and beautiful poems have appeared previously in magazines and chapbooks. But I see these poems primarily as weapons of psychic survival and only incidentally as good literature. Each man represented in these pages fought to preserve his identity, his existential wonder, his joy at being alive in the world, his rage at being imprisoned. In doing so he gave courage to others who might have abandoned the fight, might have succumbed, as so many before them had, to the darkness of not seeing, not feeling, and doing "easy time."

The Writer's Workshop which gave these men the opportunity to write was not a bold, new experiment. Things like it had been tried before in New York,

New Jersey, and California prisons. However, the purpose of those workshops was essentially an artistic one, a creative one.

When Nancy Pierce of the Arizona Commission on the Arts and Humanities proposed this particular Workshop, she had a different vision and different expectations. It was her hope that the Workshop would simply be a place behind the walls where men could go, a safe place where they could be open and honest, where they could express what they felt without intimidation or fear of reprisal. It would be a place where they could have access through books, tapes, and visits, to the best of contemporary writing in America. If nothing publishable was produced, in her mind the Workshop would not be a failure as long as it had become that kind of place for the men inside.

That the Workshop became the kind of place Nancy envisioned — in addition to a great deal more — was due to a number of factors. First among them was the enthusiasm of J. Charles Green, a young poet who died from acute hepatitis while the Workshop was still in its first year. Charlie was the anchor man, Nancy's man inside, who handled all the tedious and frustrating details such as typing memos, cellblock turnouts, and gate passes for visitors. He recruited new men for the Workshop, wrote progress reports to the Commission and to the Prison Administration, and follow-up articles for the Penal Press. That the Workshop became accepted as a *fait accompli* by the prison officials after the first summer was due in no small way to Charlie Green.

Next, there was the gentleness and wisdom of Richard Shelton, the director of the Workshop. Dick is a professor at the University of Arizona and a brilliant poet. His wife Lois is the director of the Poetry Center at the U. of A. They became the only family some guys in the Workshop ever really knew — arranging for visits, writing letters, discussing personal problems, helping on parole plans, even remembering birthdays. They are, quite simply, fine human beings.

Between the two of them we got just about any book we requested — no matter how "far out" or esoteric. If the Commission didn't have it and the University didn't have it, Dick would still manage to dig it up somewhere. He brought tape recordings of readings by William Stafford, Lucille Clifton, Mark Strand, and others from the Poetry Center. When W.S. Merwin came to Arizona, Dick brought him to the Workshop to read and also just talk to the men there. Dr. Lewis Merklin, Jr., the noted psychiatrist and author of *They Chose Honor*, came all the way from his post at the University of Pennsylvania Medical Center to rap with us. The Workshop was a happening.

But it was also a quiet place where people listened, really listened, to what you had to say. It was a place where people truly gave a damn about how you felt. No guards were there to look over your shoulder or report what was said to the front office.

I have been using the past tense because I am describing what the Workshop has been over the past four years, the period during which these poems and prose pieces were written. But it is a dynamic group which changes and grows a dozen different ways and in a dozen different directions each week. This anthology merely marks a point of celebration — not a point of arrival or departure. Simply a jumping up with joy in the middle of things to say: *See, we're alive and we're part of the world!* The Workshop continues and will continue, I hope, for many years to come.

All of us who have work in this volume are grateful for those in the Workshop who provided us with criticism, encouragement, and also, in some cases, the impetus to go on writing. Melven Taylor, a wise and talented critic, will find many echoes of his comments and suggested revisions in the poems as will many others. For those who submitted the hundreds of poems and prose pieces that reluctantly could not be used in this book, our thanks for their understanding and support in spite of personal disappointment.

Finally, it should be noted that this book is as much a product of those who have been transferred, parolled, or released as it is of those of us who remain. It is also a product of men like Charlie Green and Paul Ashley who, through illness or prison violence, did not live to see their work in print.

It is to all the men who are not here to celebrate with us that this book is dedicated.

Michael Hogan
Florence, Arizona

It appears that everything that needs to be said about the importance of such a program for a convict in a Prison has already been said extremely well and appropriately so by a convict contributor who has provided the introduction to this anthology.

While there are many struggles within a prison, both for the keeper and the kept, none is more important than mental and intellectual survival.

Certainly the Writer's Workshop has allowed some to succeed and I commend all who have taken part or contributed to its success.

— John J. Moran, Director
State of Arizona Department of Corrections

It seems to me that the value of a Writer's Workshop in a prison setting is at least two-fold: the opportunity for man to express his needs, frustrations, satisfactions, hopes, beliefs, and joys on the written page is undoubtedly of great value in helping him to know the meaning of his own life, of life in general, and the directions in which our civilization moves.

A second benefit of the Writer's Workshop seems to me to be the possibility of retaining in a very drab, confining, and sometimes emotionally charged atmosphere the human characteristics that are necessary to sustain a man's hope for a better future.

These two benefits, that of self-expression and of maintaining a human character, are in themselves valuable enough to justify and commend a Writer's Workshop.

For this worthwhile work, I commend the participants in the workshop and the leadership that has had the vision to sustain them in the preparation of this anthology.

I hope the work will be of benefit to all readers, but most especially to the inmates who have expressed themselves in it.

— John E. Wright, Deputy Warden
Department of Corrections
Arizona State Prison

Do not go gentle into that good night.
Rage, rage against the dying of the light.

Dylan Thomas

CONTENTS

ROMAN ADRIAN

My Grandfather	1
Bel Woman	2

PAUL DAVID ASHLEY (1942 – 1975)

Prison	3
The Ritual	4
All We Wanted	5
Song From The Unfinished Man	6,7
Ladies In Love	8
Beauty	9
Ending An Affair	10,11
Sounds	12,13

JIMMY SANTIAGO BACA

Three Friends Of Mine	14
Another Love Poem	15,16,17

ARLIE "FRANKO" DURHAM

Speeding	18
A Prisoner	19

JIM FARRAR

Bones Found In Chalk	20
Life Dance	21
It Is Good To Know You	22
Hokusai	22
Two Alternatives To One Moment's Experience	23
Hurrying Home	24

J. CHARLES GREEN (1947 – 1974)

Waking Up	25
Parole Denial	25
Isolation Cell Poem	26
Freedom	27
A Day Of Notes	28
A Thought In The Center Of A Memory	29
From "Arioso"	30,31
Inside The Wall Of My Cell	32,33

MICHAEL HOGAN

One Summer In Charleston 34
Passing Through Virginia 35
Groundhog Day 36
Fish 37
A Quiet Orderly Life 38
Rust 39
Christmas Poem 40
Poem For My Eighth Year In Prison 41

ROBERT T. KASOLD

Artistry 42
Prison Dorm 43
Glass Flowers In A Glass Ball 44
Happy 45

LONNIE L. LANDRUM

Racist Delicious 46
Another Commercial 46
The For Real Ghetto 47
Where Were You? 48
And Now Out Of Sight 49
Retrospect 49
Dissipation 50

DANNY LAURINO

At The Gates 51

DANA "THE MOUSE" MERKEL

Poets 52
You Got Parole 53

KENNETH "SPIDER" NICHOLSON

Diagnostic Center 54
Letter 55
A Letter Home 56

JOHN L. SELLERS

Reincarnation   57
A Historical Note   58
Marriage   59
Small Town History   60
An Army Buddy Used To Say   61

MICHAEL SMALL

A Narrow Street   62
Black Stallion   63
The Widow Of A Man Still Breathing   64
A Dream   65
Charlie 12   66
Looking For Someone   67
At Night   68
I Can Forget   69
The Bed   70
When Roots Get Too Deep   71
At The Top   72
On Being Late   73

CASH TERRELL

The Hand Of Ms. Fate   74
The Dodos   75
For My Pop   76
From The Convict's Diary — May 10th   77
From The Convict's Diary — May 12th   78
From The Convict's Diary — May 18th   79
From The Convict's Diary — May 21st   80
From The Convict's Diary — May 26th   81
Trolls   82
I Hope I Never Get There   83

JOHN T. ZAREMBA

Negotiations   84
The Profligate   85

For our brothers

ROMAN ADRIAN

MY GRANDFATHER

Oh, Lance of Lightning,
strike the Earth
making it holy.

There Thunder beats
the drum and the gods dance.
Tears come to the dryness.

Corn rising tall
in your midst.
My grandfather chants:
Hear me, Oh Sacred Messenger.
I give thanks to my Creator.

Flaming out of the Sun
and into the blueness,
through the feathers of a Rainbow,
the Eagle comes.

BEL WOMAN

Woman, I may be a stone from
    which you step up to better things.
    I don't mind.
    But during the time you linger
    here with me, the joy of you
    will be a comfort to my spirit.

Then, the day may come when you
look and the stone will be gone.
It will have broken and
sank beneath the river that you crossed.

PAUL DAVID ASHLEY

PRISON

if you would work one small miracle
repair one man
without violence or contempt
assemble one body
without leaning on the grotesque
inventions of pain

if I could understand the mystery of rain
how it holds its dignity
in the violence of a storm
if freedom was not more important
than even god or death
you could have me I would not escape

THE RITUAL

I stand below the gun tower
in the rain. Other prisoners line up.
behind me. They want to return
to their cells. "Not yet," I tell them.

"Not until the bastard
stops calling me by a number."

It is late and because visitors are present
the tower guard grudgingly calls
my name.
I walk through the gate
as if I were almost human.

Later in the darkness
he takes me from my cell.

He begins the ritual
of unconsciousness. I hear the thud
of clubs falling on flesh. When I call
out my number the guards walk
away. I shout at them.

"My name, goddam you, call me
by my name."

And they return.

4

ALL WE WANTED

what now spirit
haven't we already been there

who can explain
the eyes moving without orbit
the wars the small faces
thudding to earth

is there a sign
in the hands crowding the hours
around us the air
cooling against metal the sparrow
moving away

what does it mean
spirit

why is it easier
to hate what we are afraid of
to destroy what we can't
understand why is it

easier to turn
on the light than question the darkness
easier to invent beauty
than to find it

easier to run away
when all we wanted was someone
to give us warmth in the night

SONG FROM THE UNFINISHED MAN

who I am
holds on all sides
of me like glass
holds even
above me as if I were
a masked falcon held in a jar
I sing I beat
against the perimeter
of my madness
and still this thing leaves me here
with nowhere to go except alone

---

if I could give you anything
any of you
it would be love if I could find it
lying out there broken
in fields certain birds recognize

---

those who find love
are like those who find success
and both keep the discovery secret
as if afraid
the slightest revelation
will cause it to disappear
and who can blame them
what they found
must be rare so few of us
find it
forgive me spirit

(Song From The Unfinished Man)

as much as I am
at peace with all things
living within my reach as much
as I comb my hair differently and hold
my fingers in difficult positions
birds will not approach

LADIES IN LOVE

Ladies should never fall in love.
They become stars
no one can reach. To appear taller
they cut their heads off and stand on them.

Some carry their breasts
in gunny sacks so as not to appear
pretentious. At night they unbutton
their nerves
in front of vibrators
and stare at collections of bearded men.

Some fall in love with dark vowels
and foreign accents. At night
they can be seen talking
in taverns with dangerous criminals.
Their voices are small animals
waiting to be fed.

BEAUTY

even among the deformed
there is a certain beauty: in the hand
of an amputee
rising to ward off a blow

in those who let us
do things against their will
when they know it is something else
we really wanted

in the father whose daughter
is neither rich nor beautiful, in her
face when she realizes
we were lying
and accepts money for the first time

in the recognition
that our smallest disappointment
is still more than any of us can afford

in our words
when we continue without winning,
when even whiskey or a parachute won't set
us down easy

when we continue as if we had
broken the light
down into pieces small enough to carry,
when we continue
as if we had portioned our lives exactly

ENDING AN AFFAIR

is love the clang
a bell makes
in each of us is it the sound
heard over our heads and struck enough
times is it the vibration
killing us
is it a beautiful tone
or for many of us is it confused
with the dropping of metal on hard
surfaces like skulls

---

after saying always
how can you
leave like this aren't you afraid
the sounds of those
mad things
we did will follow you
where will you go
for warmth
sitting like a chair
in anybody's tub fitting all right
but not exactly

---

tell me what we had
between us
this quiet thing growing
too rich in soil
was it distance
why then toward the end
were we shouting
and far away

(Ending An Affair)

over love it is over
carried to the side
and dumped
into the bruised water
of our suffering and still
it is almost beautiful the light of this
strange animal feeding on my salt

SOUNDS

each night we hear the sound
of small things
breaking
is it our faith and what is that
on the bandages

———

inside each other with our shovels
we scrape the darkness evenly
into piles and burn them
turning ourselves over and over in the smoke

———

looking for comfort we feel a shudder
as if a giant bird
flew out of us
and then a small bullet
opening in our brains

———

even as we turn
pretending to sleep we hear
each other masturbating in the darkness
who are we thinking of
is anyone
thinking of us
and if they arrived how soon
would we tire of them

(Sounds)

bless us spirit bless the wolves
living in our fingers
bless those who follow until we lose
them one at a time in the snow
bless the smallest
of our deaths
even they are too much to lose

———

one death at a time
we leave for our children one death
we post naked as a lord it falls
behind us one death comes
and goes as it pleases
it is the one
we are

13

THREE FRIENDS OF MINE

Fill
my pants and shirt
with youthful flesh
behind curtains of red leafy sun,
beneath a dawn green as apple boughs.
Leaking dew
drops into the earth
like piano keys
playing a love song.
This is morning.
I am in love with you.

The sun's lemon knuckles mat the grassy foothills,
wind grinds the decayed fangs of peaks,
white-haired mountain goats drink the winds
that have come from sharpening
buffalo bones on the millstone plains,
chopping leaves off trees asleep forever.
And over the rocks
comes the autumn afternoon.
I am in love with you, too.

And from a brimming cask
of dark wine
I drink with mouth and palms
with fingers and toes
three cups of stars and one sickle moon.
Loving the night
I'll spin to sleep, to sleep,
to sleep.

ANOTHER LOVE POEM

Love
landing easily, easily caught
in ourselves
dancing on
very real in my heart

where the quivering blood
turns to a slender blossom
and your kisses ride mild
as a yellow butterfly.

The hours go by, slowly by,
until we feel the other's presence near
like elephant's feet
lumbering by the heart

then into our oval eyes
to each other
flags from tiny brown islands
that say kiss me
and in the deep rich earth of our lungs
the kisses plant themselves
giving us breath to live.

(Another Love Poem)

Our bodies burn the night
while its black gallon lips part and
love sounds from distant venus
down the linen space
down to an illusion of the sun
of us, breast to breast, mouth to mouth,
fertilizing the heart
in streams of splashing love, pure love,
until gently the dawn rolls
its whiskers across our eyelids to awake.

The leg muscles of twilight softly strain away
from our window and the morning lies
like a sleepy moth
under the warm light of sunrise.

Your footsteps carry like birdcalls
truly
your movements are in tune
with jungle drums
as you walk down the dew green road at my side.
From your bosom
soft and warm as brown chilean sands
your morning words carry up
through breath clear as spring water,
copper moons shine on your hands
and your words move to fill my ears

(Another Love Poem)

as fragrant coffee does the nose
of fishermen
out on the coastal regions where
in the vast ocean waves
crystal rafters of sunrise
float as they do in your eyes.

And though
I've never been to these places
each morning intimately
you take me there
as we walk to work,
you to dust the cold books
of freedom in the city
and I to fields that are not mine.

ARLIE "FRANKO" DURHAM

SPEEDING

My face is on fire
my legs are like wire
my mind is a burning flame.

Been up ten days
trying to figure out ways
to prove that the mirror's insane.

A PRISONER

I know a man in prison.
He believes all the world is a prison.
He cannot leave.
He is my friend.

I ask him:
Do you believe you are chained to earth?
He answers:
Yes, chained and following shadows.

I seek the stars.
I cannot fly.
I'll run this treadmill
until I die.

BONES FOUND IN CHALK

head nodding over moist dreams
i am the sea salt of my blood
i am the sigh of tides with every breath
the fanged cliff stone curving to the air
the wondering sand of the ocean's stomach

merged in sediment
locked in time's ancestral mountain
i am surely the footsteps
of neanderthal man
of the spectral-eyed lemur
of the thunder lizard
the reef-dweller blind on the ocean floor

i am swaying   not asleep

LIFE DANCE

yes, my friend
hurry to the candle flame

let its blazing light show
the other side of your hand

speed to that brittle flame of colors
corona envelops white-heart center
of its dance the flame is in your eyes

the flame is in your eyes

IT IS GOOD TO KNOW YOU

winter breaks   dissolving concrete
washing steel in green living
smoke of grass   clouds roll in blue

breaking over the sun
breaking over my forehead

holding great tao in my hand
smiling silent

HOKUSAI

old friend
i saw one brown ricepaper print
from your prolific art
lying in a glass storefront

what were you doing there
among the ducks and watermelons

TWO ALTERNATIVES
TO ONE MOMENT'S EXPERIENCE

when the rose is slowing
over its belly's ample explosion
when one body explores newly
vacant bed's still warmth
and slim leaves mimic oysters
surrounding lost milk glass beads
and the hand captures three
drops of light within belly hair

soft mouth questioning night
opens in slow astonishment
and eyelids quicken to a door's
explosion and the mouth opens
to a slow growth of questions
to a new day's quickening eye

HURRYING HOME

because there is no time to rest
the sun will halt obligingly
behind the roots of mountains

and i won't return to where
rivers halt and turn to valleys
or pull up the roots of things to see
where earthy veins feed the lawns of grass

i can't forget memories left behind like old bones

because there will be time to sleep
the reddening sun's hair
will cover snowy mountain peaks

and i won't wait for highways to be built
or halt to gape at darkening space
quickening, quickening
the path rushes beneath

i will arrive in time

WAKING UP

I put my sweatshirt
on backwards this morning.
A billion sparks of stars
flowed from my mouth.

PAROLE DENIAL

today there are holes in
the air
i go in and
out

i have lost my
stomach
among dead fish

ISOLATION CELL POEM

in here
the gods have lost all their words
and i am incapable
of creating new sounds
to keep myself company

i breathe in deeply
the closeness of my body
while the air
like dead skin
breathes blood into the darkness
almost as if it could rejuvenate
a voice gone silent for centuries

and just supposing the air could speak again
which of us would first bite our tongues
asking forgiveness of the other?

FREEDOM

my cellpartner quick
turns his head from my eyes
before mumbling that being free
can't be touched by his hands

now the night has given birth
to layers of ice
in places where the summer
used to store muddied pools of rain
to hide the sun from children

A DAY OF NOTES

(that fit into the puzzle
of a poem)

1.
on the athletic field
with a hot sun
ignorant of its intrusion
into the holes of skin

so hot even syllables melt
much as the seas of salt
collected on my shirt

2.
off in a corner
unaware of anyone's eyes
sits an aged con
speaking to a young guard
as intricately as the silence
which passes in conversation
at the touching of a lover's hand

and from the old man's chest
a tattooed butterfly
seems to take flight
with the tired movement of a cough

3.
inside my chest
there is this kind of total feeling

yeah
like a child who is laughing
because it's winter's last night

A THOUGHT IN THE CENTER
OF A MEMORY

I wanted to make love with you
that night in the cocoon of your sleeping bag at Soldier's Field
but your "No" was so much the frightened innocence
of a gentle deer running from your eyes
and I could not persist into the forest of your fear.

And the damned cars racing by at the swan hour of 3 a.m.
leaving echoes of their destination in Sabino Canyon.
Because of them I was for once really St. George
with my sword of rushing wind
upon my stallion of rocks protecting you.

There were no sinners anywhere that night.
And good and evil were exactly what they are:
two words we use to describe nothing.
What there was hiding in the womb of dark sleeplessness
was the birth of two people needing each other.

From "ARIOSO"

I call on the sun to strip
us naked
until our faces melt
our bones crumble
our flesh is carried off by ants building
metropolises of seaweed
our nerves
become violins playing Requiem Masses
for newborn philosophers
our hair
strings hearts and entrails to forever
and we stand
eyeless bodyless boneless muscleless hairless
we stand in churches
and temples of earth
we stand beneath mountains
we cannot speak
we are being only
we possess
nothing.
Let the love we speak of possess us
if you are willing to be its bodyguard
to ward off the injuries of indifference.

(From "Arioso")

O, my friend
keep giving even when they smash the gifts
into your skull
and laugh as they walk away.
It is their politics.
Don't let it hurt you.
Be braver than they are
than they who are so weak
they can't accept your gentleness.
It is their way of running from themselves
Sing! Sing!
with your dancing movements of growth.

INSIDE THE WALL OF MY CELL

I sit on a discarded army bunk that moves toward death
facing a wall two feet away
facing the departure of a thousand years of dreams.

Keeper of the keys.
Gaoler.
I favor these older terms
grown older than cliches.
The punishment is the same
they feed your brain to blistered stomachs
chain your eyes to cockroaches
open the whip wounds on your back with mock seriousness
and laugh as your hands fly away
beneath the guillotine of their indifference.

Come here at 3 a.m. to my cell
with your hundred keys
poking dogs' eyes howling music
and stand inside the wall with me
which never leaves to follow you
down lost roads to your towns
made with shackled dreams.

(Inside The Wall Of My Cell)

Inside the wall
we will be brothers
nakedly
crying for drunken fathers and
masturbating fantasies of young girls
sans training bras
in black leather and nine foot whipping tongues
whispering love to each other.
I would kiss your knees
and hold your hands to my throat
to share a mother's need with you.
I would be your repressed masochism
your stolen servant.

In the wall brothers can exist as
all else fades melting into rivers of urine
sucked into their stomachs
like transparent
vapor trails across the retina.

An intrepid child is walking by
bending down
hurling
eternity in the wrong direction.

MICHAEL HOGAN

ONE SUMMER IN CHARLESTON

Not far from the Cooper River Bridge
this cornfield ends in marshland.
A solitary crow goes there and returns.
This morning, children from our farm,
heavy with rubber boots and light with wonder,
venture into the marsh.

There is a woman near the old cyprus.
They find her, fish underbelly white and bloated,
and what they do is expected.
It is what children do with dead things —
a skunk, a gutted dog by a highway.
They poke her with sticks and the sharp
points of their curiosity. She does not bleed.
A cloud of blueflies vibrates above her.

Her jump from the bridge has come to this:
not resting quietly in that graveyard of beer cans
and clam shells beneath the bridge,
but floating face down in the marsh.
The police know the whole story of
how the darkness of her husband's death
was like the tide which brought her to this spot.
So they ask the children only what
they need to know of time and place.

But the children have more of a story to tell:
how the fish nibbled away at the big toe,
how her auburn hair floated red and
green among the duckweed.
She floats now in some of their dreams
face down and heavy with darkness.

PASSING THROUGH VIRGINIA

The boy balanced on the big root
watching the helicopter seeds of maples
spin like dying insects
is waiting for life to begin.
He doesn't suspect his green eyes
are more alive
than those speeding by him in cars.

It is difficult to learn
not to be waiting and thinking:
surely the best days of my life
are yet to be lived somewhere else
any place but this
is where love is and where
life will truly begin.

The crickets know nothing of such things.
Out behind the garage in the high grass
searching among the helicopter wrecks
of spun-out maple seeds
they sing lustily of this day
for the summer that is all their lifetime.

GROUNDHOG DAY

So here we are again
looking out from our burrows.
The spring air is sharp
and sweet as arterial blood.
Beneath us, the rumpled earth is warm
with winter sleep.

We will not come forth from the burrows today.
Having lain so long in its warmth,
the darkness has a claim on us
and is reluctant to let us go.

Our folk tales tell how one of our young
(on a day much like this)
ventured forth in the sun full of high aspirations.
When he returned half-blinded,
lost to himself and the darkness,
he could not name a single shadow.

We who have lost everything else
know darkness has its consolations.
Here, there is the quiet worship of our dead
kissing the earth with dry lips.
Here, the meaning of all shadows.

FISH

The kid's packed the last five months
of his old lady's letters
in a Cherry Tyme box rolled up
in his mattress along with a towel
and now he's moving from the tank
to A-run scared and winking
at some big dude.
Tonight he'll tell his whole life story
to someone sitting on the bottom bunk
and the dude
(maybe the same one he winked at)
will watch the way the kid's hair
falls gently down over one eye,
trying to catch a swish in the voice.
In a month the kid will have
a locker full of tailormades, new shoes,
special-pressed blues,
and no room at all for a Cherry Tyme box
with letters from a face he can't remember.

A QUIET ORDERLY LIFE

The old man's been deadlocked there
in the same basement cell
for six and a half years.
Even the guards can't remember why.
Every day he does two hundred pushups
and runs fifteen miles in place.
He offers himself occasional words of encouragement
and dresses each night in his cleanest blues.
It is a quiet orderly life
and the guard captain says
the old man is content there
and doesn't like to be distrubed.

RUST

The bars on my cell have rusted.
It is intriguing to think how that happened.

Less than a decade ago they were forged
of the finest tempered steel.
They were dipped in great vats, coated with primer,
set in place with torches
then sprayed with institutional green.

Now they've rusted.

It is incredible to think that this
has occurred in the desert.
There is no moisture to speak of.
On autumn mornings dust covers the leaves,
not frost.
Most years it rains only twice in the summer.

Have there been, I wonder, little people
chipping away at the paint,
oxidizing the metal with damp diminutive hands?
Late, late at night when the walls have cooled,
it is all I can do to resist the urge
to search in the darkness beneath my bunk
where there could be a mushroom, pale and mysterious,
growing out of the concrete floor.

CHRISTMAS POEM

Sparrows drift over the mess hall
like smoke from a charcoal fire.
It is cold.
Steam rises from a sewer cover
touching my face with blue fingers.
Behind me others follow:
poor, blind children asking for what they want,
given what they deserve.

Dubbed with the blunt of that same sword
I do not stop to congratulate myself
or weep any longer over the bodies of my brothers,
their words unwinding like fuses
toward some final explosion the other side of the wall.
Their love like damp fingers
is cold against my ribs.

Fate had three children: two were born crippled.
The third holds a handful of love
like coal in his stocking.

POEM FOR MY EIGHTH YEAR IN PRISON

We name a thing and then we know it,
take possession and make it ours.
Poverty, I name you "freedom"
and I am free.
This cell in my eighth year I call "solitude"
and the darkness doesn't betray me.
The days I call "now"
and do not count them.
There is only one "now" not several.

My past binds the keepers more securely
than me.
It is, more than mine, their prison.
This life, which is neither mine nor theirs
but that of the world,
I call "a green and growing thing"
and the swallows come from miles around
to build their nests.

ROBERT T. KASOLD

ARTISTRY

As Aubry worked by candles
and Edgar by the bottle
So I compose by roaches —
the three I've had to throttle.

PRISON DORM

As magicians' swords pierce wicker baskets
    so floodlights storm our windows
    catching us in their crossfire.

Awake, we are on guard
    but to sleep is to be vulnerable.
In the troubled silence someone grinds his teeth.

A match glow is born,
    dies in a breath.
And my thoughts are bigger than the night.

GLASS FLOWERS IN A GLASS BALL

Here we are, inside.
    Inside.
Our sky is one unchanging
    silvered sphere.
To try to see the world
    is to see but our own image
    reflected inward.

Are we never again to feel
    the gentle rain?
What good are flowers forever sealed?
    Beauty never touched?
Are we now so fragile
    that to be freed
    would be our destruction?

I shout: Is anyone out there
    aware I'm here?
Do you still exist?
    Do I?

HAPPY?

— To Mary

Yes, I am happy for you
      that you have found someone
      that you will share each other.

Being happy with someone is best
      but being happy for them
      is better than not being happy at all.

LONNIE L. LANDRUM

RACIST DELICIOUS

Take four hundred years of exploitation
Add four chopped centuries of genocide.
Sprinkle lightly with strange fruit.
Mix well
With thirty million varieties of depressed
Niggas.
Put contents into ghetto container.
Shake well until fermented.
You may buy ingredients
Wherever
Amerikkkan products
Are sold.

ANOTHER COMMERCIAL

Amerikkka
The beautiful
Has a funky
Breath.
Listerine
Keeps
Her mouth clean.
But
How she gonna
Wash
Her nasty
Polluted
Ass?

THE FOR REAL GHETTO

Yeah, you remember the ghetto,
The funky ghetto,
Where Niggas cut, shoot and fight
One another every night.
In the ghetto where
Hustlin's a life style
And even as a kid
You ain't shit
Till you been to juvenile.
In the ghetto, the junky ghetto,
Where there's a thousand vices and sins
And you momma might have to turn a trick
To meet ends.
Yeah, you remember the ghetto
Where you was born
To a jive motherfucker who left home
To resign life for a bottle of wine.
On the corner in the ghetto
Where ain't a damn thing changed
Since the first peckerwood
Invented capitalistic gain.
In the ghetto
Where there's filth, junk and pollution
And Niggas bad-mouthin' honkys as the solution.
In the ghetto
Where Niggas live, Niggas die.
Niggas kill, Niggas survive
And slowly transform into *black folks*
In the ghetto.

WHERE WERE YOU?

Where were you
When the Mayflower arrived?
Where were you
When the sea brought the tide?
Where were you
As I toiled in the sun?
Where were you
When massa ripped out my tongue?
Where were you
When my grass hut was cold?
Where were you
When my man-child was sold?
Where were you
As I screamed out your name?
Where were you
When my screams were in vain?
Where were you
God?
Where *WERE* you?

AND NOW OUT OF SIGHT

Brought to Amerikka
To fulfill her dreams
Our work has been finished
But we don't own a thing
And our job is not done.
And I have assumed
If progress continues
We'll be slaves on the moon.
So don't be surprised
If you wake in the night
Buckling your seat belt
In a nuclear satellite.
From Africa to Amerikka
And now
     out
        of
          sight!

RETROSPECT

Watching the astronauts
Go to the moon
On my deserved
     1965 Watts T.V.,
Visualizing the 1619 slave craft, *Mayflower,*
Smoking my down to earth marijuana.
Hummmmmmmmmmmnnnnnnn
       Bye
          Bye
            Black
              Bird!

DISSIPATION

I've wished a million times
We could speak
Our ancestral tongue
Or even know the village, tribe
Or town that we come from.

Don't you miss, deep in your soul,
The language we once knew?

To describe the world in Congolese
Would be a world anew.

Is there a way of getting back
What was taken from our soul?
Until we speak our mother tongue
We never will be whole.

DANNY LAURINO

AT THE GATES

All things come to him who waits:
$100 dinners on silver plates.
Tomatoes come in wooden crates
and the man in prison masturbates.

DANA "THE MOUSE" MERKEL

POETS

I watch them
producing their work like
laborers unloading freight from
some dark boxcar interior
apparently
unconcerned with
the complexity of the marvels
they bring into the light
and I feel alien to the scene
one who sees
but does not comprehend
as though the latest arrival
has aroused me from my place
beneath a bridge by the freight-yard
to gaze
resentment filling
my crusty eyes.

YOU GOT PAROLE

Sure are sorry to
see ya go not really
but you know how it
is and i'm happy to
see you go only i'm gonna
miss yer dumb smile
and how when yer talkin
i never know when yer
gonna say somethin smart
or stupid and how i wish
even though i love ya
it wuz me goin not you.

DIAGNOSTIC CENTER

With the surgical hands
    of a garbage collector
The skilled training
    of a moron
They begin to pick
    your brain.
Welcome
    to the prison diagnostic center.

LETTER

Dear Sir,
    You're a pig
        Your wife's a pigstress
    And your children piglets.

                Sincerely,
                    Spider

55

A LETTER HOME

You say you love me
but you wouldn't spit to help me.
Were our situations reversed
I'd have given my life to help you.
You write: a son has an obligation of love.
And I reply: Why don't you shit in your back pocket
and sit on it?

JOHN L. SELLERS

REINCARNATION

Of all the birds I love,
I would rather be a duck.
I would swim along the river bank,
And watch the people fish.

Of all the fish I love,
I would rather be a bass.
I would climb upon the slippery rocks,
and slide down on my hands and knees.

Of all the animals I love,
I would rather be a skunk.
I would spray all the so-called poets
Who write this type of junk.

A HISTORICAL NOTE

(From George Washington To His Father)

Father, I cannot tell a lie,
It was I who chopped the cherry tree down.
I wanted to bake a cherry pie
but all the stores were closed in town
because it was my birthday.

MARRIAGE

Marriage within the group is endogamy
And outside the group it's exogamy
And bigamy is the practice of polygamy
And polygamy is polyandry or polygyny
But monogamy is monotony.

SMALL TOWN HISTORY

George Grover was the town looney. He had been caught peeping in windows a few times but he was considered harmless and nobody bothered him until the night Old Man MacMillan caught him fucking his nanny goats. They sent George to the State Hospital and MacMillan's milk business dropped to zero so he sold all his goats. Two years later George was released from the hospital but he never came back to town. The rumor going around was that he had a job up in Utah herding sheep.

AN ARMY BUDDY USED TO SAY

Hold your head high,
Look 'em in the eye,
And smile when you die.

When I asked him why
I should smile when I die,
This was his reply:

It drives on-lookers mad
From curiosity.

MICHAEL SMALL

A NARROW STREET

it wouldn't be so damn bad
but five cold mornings each week
i stand on this same corner
waiting for bus number 15
which hasn't been on time once
in the three years
i've worked for palmer & son
even miss colleri
doesn't appeal to me anymore
she wears the same wind song
that lately
smells like a pest repellent
and besides her skirts
never got any shorter
she did have a nice behind
but you know how sitting on your ass
all day tends to make hips spread
and there's that new account
the boss has put me on
my first solo
maybe that's why i'm so uptight
or is it because
my god my fucking god
nobody ever told me what to do
if the bus doesn't come

BLACK STALLION

you gallop
and the wind runs
at your side
i close my eyes
to bring you close to me
your eyes pierce me
as a child's eyes
your mane flows from your neck
as grass from good ground
your legs carry the sheik
that is your body

in the silence of your dust
as i put my rope away
i know there are few like you
and many like me

THE WIDOW OF A MAN
WHO IS STILL BREATHING

it was some time between the 6th grade
and your first cigarette
when you left me for the first time

now you hide from me
behind a wall of what
everyone you know
might think of me

i sleep on the couch
you are too drunk too tired
you have a headache

when you are alone
you flirt with me
but you sleep with someone else
who is socially acceptable

i can never tell when you are listening
but if you are i promise
wherever you go i will be close by
just in case you ever change your mind

even knowing it will likely be death
who takes me back before you will
cannot change who i am
i was made for you
i am the dream you had of being yourself

A DREAM

i stood over myself
with a whip of talons
and flogged myself
with the opinions of others
until one night
as i tossed in a half sleep
i read an autobiography
written in my own hand
the first page was the usual
it said i was born
the second page found me
in a cold sweat wide awake
it said i had died
cause of death
severe and repeated beatings
self-inflicted

CHARLIE 12

there are no cracks in the wall
this house is full of smaller ones
there are searchlights with loud voices
gun barrels with eyes

i have come to know my house
but it was not easy
it was cold at first
and would not speak to me
now we talk all night

my house knows everything about me
my thoughts leapfrog on the walls
my dreams are stains in a coffee cup
my silence is carved with a date
next to the mirror

my hope is gripping the door
TURNKEY TURNKEY
CHARLIE 12

LOOKING FOR SOMEONE

i walk down
a street paved with hollow faces
no one walks with me
i run down
an alley towering in darkness
no one can catch me
i swim naked
in a river of my own blood
no one can see me

as i walk
the wind is where i was
whispering to my shadow that i have gone
as i run
nothing is where i was
dripping like a wet memory on the desert
as i swim
death is where i am
touching my hand and crusting my eyes

someone
someone lies next to me
i have been too busy dying to see
anyone but me
now my shadow sits on the corner
and i stand across the street
without even a shadow
looking for someone
anyone
to fill the emptiness
despair has breathed deep into me

AT NIGHT

all things find a place
to wait
all things move slowly
and only of necessity

the moon carries my silence
there is no one to hear my voice
telling lies about who i am

I CAN FORGET

when i am asleep

when the woman i love
is loving me

when the dog
and the children next door
are quiet so i can sleep

when the trees
are webbed with autumn

sometimes i can forget
i am being followed
by the shadows i have been

THE BED

the night
empty as a condemned house

the trees
slapping the windows
where there are no lights

the dark wind
climbing my back

the cold bed
whose breath mists the darkness
whose voice calls softly
to those who are alone
and is heard only by those
who can bear it

WHEN ROOTS GET TOO DEEP

there was a seed
and when the rain came
it became a blade of grass
part of it grew up into the wind
and part of it took root

at night
when it is sure no one is watching
it grows
it has a dream

when it is cut it bleeds
and it is greener
covered with the blood of dreams

i am like the grass
part of me is always somewhere else
and part of me grows deeper

when roots get too deep
and i no longer dream
i will turn brown and die

AT THE TOP

i had never been to the top of anything
so as i climbed the stairs
it was difficult to keep up with my anticipation
i thought the sky would be longer
the sun would be kinder
the birds would be more than wings

the sky was longer
but my eyes grew weary of the distance
the sun was kinder
but i never let anything get too close to me
the birds even had voices
and i called to them
but they did not answer

then since i was out of a dream
i had to come down

ON BEING LATE

i was late for today
and i ran after it

yesterday i was late
and the day before
each time i'm late
i swear it won't happen again

i think what is it
always makes me late
and realize
my life is a book
already written
my death the page
i won't ever read

CASH TERRELL

THE HAND OF MS. FATE

Now listen closely, children. Quiet now. Quiet, I said! Johnny, you take your feet down off that desk this minute! Very well, now listen. This is the day I promised to assign your futures to you so we'll get to that right away. I'll read off each of the openings and then, if there's one that interests you, raise your hand. Put your hand down, Johnny! You'll get your turn. Now then Suzy, which did you say? Oh yes, you'll do fine as an actress, all those pretty blond curls. What's that? Okay, it's the university for you, David. Oh my, what a perfect future for you, Annette. That was a very good choice. I'm not going to tell you any more, Johnny, and just for that you can wait until last! Fine, that's a wonderful future for you, Dennis, and that agile mind of yours will work well for you in that profession. Now then, does everyone have a future? No, I don't mean you, Johnny. Well, let me see. What's left now? Engineer? No, Johnny. Why must you be so aggressive? Oh yes, here's one that would do very nicely for you. Now stop that silly crying, Johnny. What's that? No, silly boy, you won't need to wear striped clothing, they don't do that anymore. Class dismissed.

THE DODOS

for Isaac Asimov

They are not extinct
and will return, I think,
piloting mythical chariots through skies
of their own design
to light in our midst like handed falcons
and run out jewelled stairways
demanding they be paved in garlands
made of shredded hearts
stained with the white first blood of virgins
for proof of our joy in their coming.

So if you are there
you may raise your stained face from the dust
and laugh silently
from the hollow space that held your heart
at the way their lower beaks
flap about like tongues of idiots
and at the way they giggle
over their own shadows
but be certain you cower
at the fierceness of their rheumy eyes
and pretended stature
for theirs is the vanity of gods
and you are their creation
in their image of themselves.

FOR MY POP

Who in his thirties
got out before the rooster
to work fourteen hours
at old Creech's sawmill
and would whip it out
on the last board he'd made that day,
saying, as he pondered the spread of yellow stain,
"I hope they make a table outter that 'un
an' some rich bastid has to eat offen 'er ehva day."
Then stop by Roy Mullins' still
to bring me thick-tongued stories
apologizing to mama at the end of each.

From **The Convict's Diary**
MAY 10th — THE HOLE

Today, I am troubled by the slot in my door. It is my umbilicus and everytime it opens, I feel like someone is smearing shit on my heart. The first time it opened somebody's voice wanted to know if I was still in here. "Still in there, Boy?" it said. I feel better now, **they** know I'm still in here. The next time it opened, the voice said, "Chow!" and I stole the time from its wrist when it shoved my food through. That only confused me though, because I didn't know which five o'clock it was ten minutes until. I made it easy for myself and decided it didn't matter. And this time they left my slot open and I don't know what to do about that. Maybe I should yell at them about it, because if I don't, they might think I did it some way. I think I'll look out there and see if I can tell what went wrong. Hey! there's another door over there and it looks just like mine & it has a slot & it's open. So, I guess everything is alright & I wonder why that dude over there is looking at me. "Hey, man," he says, "I see they left your slot open, too." There's a fat-assed cockroach edging its way down his door & I hear somebody's radio playing a song about how everything is beautiful in its own way & I wonder if my slot looks like his on the other side & if I ever walk past another mailbox I'm gonna push a hamburger in its slot because you can never tell . . .

77

From **The Convict's Diary**
MAY 12th — THE HOLE

I was here eight years ago and I didn't know it until I began reading my wall and found my name scratched there. All the other names are still there. I read them last time. There are some new ones, too. Like: "Jimmy from Albuquerque. Doing 5-7 for Burglary" and "Juan Flores from Cleveland. 1963-1968." The last one didn't say **why**. And then there is **his** name where I found it those years ago scratched confidently in the corner. "I am Banquet," he wrote, "doing it all. 1933 till — ." And I think of all the other places I have found his legend scratched like that. Once, on a scrap of stucco from a gone-in-1961 cellhouse. Another time in a dried-in-1953 sidewalk. And eight times in the concrete corners of cells he and I have occupied. He with his 1933 till . . . And me with my forty years later till . . .

And I remember the last place I found his name. It was chiseled in granite and someone else put it there for him.

From **The Convict's Diary**
MAY 18th — THE HOLE

> ... and said, "You who are full of all
> deceit and fraud, you son of the devil,
> you enemy of all righteousness, will
> you not cease to make crooked the
> straight ways of the Lord?"
>
> Acts 13:10

I wanted someone to talk to today so I picked an argument with the guard for slamming the flap on my slot when he came around to feed me a while ago. He explained to me that he had to shut it hard in order for it to stay closed and we talked about how it could have been designed in such a way to make it better and he closed it in my face about ten times to see if what we had thought of would work. Then, when I got tired of that I told him I was sorry for bothering him about it and would he please ask the new dude in number eight if he wanted to trade his box of cereal for my spider. He said he did and made the exchange for us and asked me how many times that made and I told him I thought it was about six and he told me that was pretty good and left.

Now, I'm sitting here waiting for my spider to come back through that ventilator duct. She has about thirty little ones over there.

From **The Convict's Diary**
MAY 21st — THE HOLE

I read some more stories from "It's the only thing you're gonna get to read for the next thirty days, Boy" today. When I got to page 391 I found out that one of those longhairs had wasted a whole bunch of dudes with the jawbone of somebody's ass. Then, just as I was trying to figure out how much time he would have gotten in the Clark County Superior Court for that, a guard came by to see if I was still in here. He saw what I was doing and suggested I read the one about a Beard named Moses. So I started in on that one and, just as I got to the part where he was leading all those people through the parting waters, the jerk in the next Hole flushed his commode and scared the living hell out of me.

From **The Convict's Diary**
MAY 26th — THE HOLE

I've had twenty-four straight hours of nothing-but-night and they're not going to turn on my light again for another twenty-four. "That what you get for acting up," they said. The dude in No. 5 caused it all. He was flushing his commode at the rate of fourteen times a minute and I couldn't stand it so I got up and flushed mine a whole lot longer to drown him out. Anyway I'd like to see that in the rule book. "No inmate may activate the water facility in his living area more than two-hundred (200) times in any twenty-four (24) hour period." Probably. Anyway, it looks to me like they could have turned the water off instead of the lights. But, I suppose they knew what they were doing because ten minutes after the lights went out they brought me three letters.

TROLLS

Sometimes if you look close enough
you can find their doors
hidden behind forgotten gravestones
whose legends they have taken
as images for their lightest verse.

At others, you may find them
in the hollowed space
beneath your child's footprint
tracing your ancestry
to infinity
explaining nothing.

And on certain nights
when a frightened wind has had its song
and left
you may enter one of these doors
letting your courage push the darkness before you
like a miner's lamp
allowing you to examine exhibitions
of their proudest works:
a child's fear
a torn life
a broken hope
and the title of your finest poem
hanging like a whore's light
over a carnival booth.

I HOPE I NEVER GO THERE

There is a place I know
where you can hear the crying
of soft blue stones
when a thieving wind comes by
on burglar's feet
to carry off all their children
for the building of its magic dunes.

Where you can buy the only ticket
in a final sweepstakes
its grand prize, a look
through the album of time
and its index marking in night
the silent pages holding your last hour.

And should it come
that you are found there,
there are two conditions to be met
before leaving is allowed.
First, you must have lost your way
to some other place
thinking to repossess it from this one.
And second, you must,
before you pass through the seventh door
place your right hand like a monkey's cup
before you,
offering all that is left of yourself
to faith.

JOHN T. ZAREMBA

NEGOTIATIONS

One amber dexterous day
when the sun was a spider web
south of the Inequity
I spindled a contrite cat
out of his last dozen tambourines.

"That's a paradox!" he exclaimed
in crystal clear anguish,
ringing his scony little heart.

"Paraducks, blackbird or swallow,
they're all the same to me
when I'm south of the Inequity.
Besides, I don't think it's a paraducks;
it's more a paragram
as any fool can plainly see."

"Well," said the cat, "the Ireland of it all!
Don't be so Finlandish; just eat your tambourines."

THE PROFLIGATE

Where once proud scarecrows stood
guarding my seeds
my manicured fields,
now only remnants in a wasteland
remain, grooves and crags,
and the seeds never grew.

The leaves, the terrible leaves,
brown harlequins, whirling
dervishes, assassins,
and the time lost in autumn.

Now I crouch like a miser
straining to retrieve fragments,
less than a dream,
searching for some small seed
of my youth
while in the distance
the heckle of young crows
in the wind,
and the seeds never grew.